bash

neil labute

BROADWAY PLAY PUBLISHING INC
224 E 62nd St, NY NY 10065-8201
212 772-8334 fax: 212 772-8358
BroadwayPlayPub.com

bash

© Copyright 1999 by neil labute

I S B N: 978-0-88145-613-4

First printing: December 2014
This printing: February 2016

Book design: Marie Donovan
Page make-up: Adobe Indesign
Typeface: Palatino
Printed and bound in the U S A

CONTENTS

bash premiered in new york city at the douglas
fairbanks theater, produced by eric krebs and
stephen pevner, on 24 june 1999. the cast and creative
contributors were as follows:

iphigenia in orem

young man .... ron eldard

a gaggle of saints

john ....paul rudd
sue ....calista flockhart

medea redux

woman ....calista flockhart

director..joe mantello
scenic design .... scott pask
costume design... lynette meyer
lighting design...james vermuelen
sound design... red ramona

for emma, chet, and billie

iphigenia in orem

(silence. darkness)

(lights up slowly to reveal a young man, early 30s, dressed in a plain suit.)

(he is seated on the edge of a hotel chair and nurses a water glass in one hand.)

YOUNG MAN: ...i'll tell it once. one time because it deserves to be told, and then never again, fair enough? well, doesn't really matter what you think, i mean, i care, i do, i want you to listen to this, hear me out, but it's not really important how you feel about it all in the end...it's happened now. and i don't know you from adam...or eve, for that matter. *(laughs)* sorry, i'm just trying to keep this... yeah, anyway, your drink okay? there's plenty over on the counter there, so feel free...the looser the better on this one, i figure, so bottoms up, or whatever they say at the bar these days. i wouldn't know. really, feel free...comes with the room. *(beat)* i'm not a drinker...you probably guessed that, though, right? yeah...nothing but water here. *(holds up glass)* never was, but when i saw you down in the lounge i could tell right away that you enjoyed the stuff, what is that you've got there? some kind of red, what, wine, is it? looks like it. wine. do, really, feel at home, all that's just gonna go to waste if you don't...well, the next person'll drink it maybe, but you know what i mean. myself, i hate to waste things... *(beat)* so anyway, when i spotted you, alone like you were and going through that bottle, i figured you'd be a great listener, that you wouldn't mind if

i told you all this…and if i'm lucky, by tomorrow,
you won't even remember it. i'm kidding, but you're
okay, comfortable? good. *(beat)* so…where should i…
let me see. alright, i never used to travel, pretty much
stayed in our branch office, did things over the phone,
handled it all that way. you know? never cared much
for driving all the time, meeting clients, that end of
things…i mean, i did it when i first started, low man
on the pole and whatever, but once i got the old m.b.a.,
foot in the door and all…i stuck to the desk as much as
i could, i like it. that office…i don't know…"feel". the
atmosphere. faxes coming in, people zipping around,
emergency strategy sessions, all that. it's like being a
kid again, playing at "war" or that type of thing, i don't
mean exactly like that, but you know what i'm saying,
it's a whole different thing out there, i have to tell
you. the world of business, it is. all that "dog eat dog",
"jungle out there" stuff has become pretty cliché now,
but it's true. i mean, you can see what guys love about
it. and i don't mean just guys either, because there's
plenty of women in the field, too, obviously, but i mean
"guys" like in…well, "guys". you know, how it's used
these days. all encompassing, it's very high stakes,
lots of cash floating around you, and the pressure's a
real…well, just hot. day in and out. seriously, it is. we
may play it like a game sometimes, but believe me, a
day doesn't go by in business that you're not out for
somebody's blood…

(pause)

but, hey, you know what i'm talking about…you're in
what, sales? yeah, i thought so. you look like… well,
no, i mean it in a complimentary…you just look like
you could sell. things, if you wanted to…

(pause)

i guess the point i'm making is that it's a stress-filled
situation i'm in, but i'm paid for it, not complaining, i
just wanted to, i don't know, lead in the right way on
this. i'm not making excuses. i'm not... *(beat)* looks like
i'm losing you. las vegas isn't that far from...must be
getting late. i'll try and be...brief—things took a bit of
a turn for us last year. well, i guess about two years
ago, now. my wife and me, the family, you know...we
lost a child, newborn, well, five months old...just like
that. just happened. *(beat)* i was off that day, a friday, i
think, and deborah, that's my wife, deb, she was out—
her mother was staying with us, and they were over at
safeway getting some milk—deb put the baby down,
"emma" we'd named her, she put emma in our bed
because that's where she'd been sleeping the first few
months...we always thought that was a good bonding
thing, i'd read it somewhere, or she heard it at church
or something like that...anyway, so that's what she
did. she tucks her in, and out they went. and see, i was
gonna lie down with her, i really was, but i just went
back into the living room for a second, watch a little
wheel of fortune or some thing, you know, five minutes
a week to myself, and i fell. fell off to sleep right there,
there on the loveseat by the window. *(beat)* deb's
mom...emma's grandma...found her. maybe a half
hour later, she'd smothered herself under the covers,
i don't know, beneath the weight of the comforter or
whatever it was. this big old maroon and gold thing
we'd gotten as a wedding gift, huge—and she'd, well,
she'd suffocated, that's about as plain as you can tell
it, right? the little thing...died in our bed, tangling
herself in the blankets. *(beat)* the police had to come,
they do for any kind of infant death, that's what the
officer said; i'd gotten a hold of myself by that time,
still crying, but deb...deb was just kind of sitting there
next to me, staring off, and this guy—this person—a
detective, i suppose, was asking us questions, standing

there and firing off this series of questions. "standard
procedure", he assured us, but still…

(pause)

what bothered him…no, "puzzled" him, he said,
never came right out and said it bothered him but
you could see by the way he…he didn't understand
how the baby could get so far down. *(beat)* now i am
losing you, right? okay, yeah, i'm getting ahead of
myself…it seemed to him that the baby, a baby that
young and small, she was such a small little thing…
was too far down toward the foot of the bed, and
turned, something about that seemed to be eating at
him. i didn't understand what he was getting at, the
way he kept going back and forth over the events and
times and all that, "where were you standing?" and
"approximately how long were you…?" blah, blah,
blah. i mean, my god, we're sitting there on the edge of
the sofa, the bed my daughter has just died in i can see
through an open door back down the hallway, and this
man is pacing around, sucking on the chewed cap of a
ballpoint pen and…asking me quietly, "did you check
on her?" *(beat)* what's he getting at, anyway? i mean,
that's a no-win, isn't it? think about it…if i didn't check
on her, i'm not a good father, not anything he can
say about it, but i carry around the guilt, you know…
maybe i could've prevented it. right? and if i did go in
there, if i had've done what i was supposed to do, had
planned on doing, the nap…then maybe she'd be alive,
maybe. *(beat)* and for just a second, just the briefest of
moments…i catch deb looking over at me. as if this is
the first time the thought's come to her as well. this
possibility, the whole incident hangs there—probably
only two or three seconds all together—but it just lays
there in the air over us all. this shadow of a doubt…
there's another cliché for you…it hangs there until i
say, very matter-of-factly, "umm, no, i didn't, i meant

to, but..." and off he goes. says "fine", stops me cold,
and off he goes. onto another tangent... *(beat)* she took
my hand in hers, deb did, just after that. scooped it up
into her tiny fingers and held it there...all the rest of
that afternoon, even after the police were gone, as we
sat there into the evening with her mother, our two
other children, home from school and having heard
it all...none of us talking, just sitting and watching
the darkness crowd into the room...she held onto my
hand. and somehow, because of that, i felt at peace...
(beat) anyway, the detective said that he was nearly
done, just one or two more items, when deborah
grabbed hold of my hand like she did. when she did
that...

(pause)

all during this i can see guys passing—oops, i mean
"people" —i can see these people passing in front
of the doorway, i could, deb was just off to the side
enough to miss it, thank heavens...tweezers all out,
picking up scraps of whatever, the snap! of flashbulbs,
some muffled talk about an upcoming jazz game...i'm
starting to feel queasy. the heat of the room, maybe,
and the sitting there as this almost unbearable thing
unfolds in front of us...we'd hardly had a moment to
hold each other, deborah and myself, to cry and, you
know, just...and this happens. this *dragnet* episode
takes place right in our living room...and i start to
feel sick. i did. i hide it pretty well, but i felt it all the
same...

(pause)

and finally they were gone. i looked around, and the
front door slammed shut and it was empty. the house,
they'd taken emma out with them, the coroner, maybe
a half hour before, wrapped in a little zip-up bag,
something like what i carry my pressed shirts in when

i travel, i mean, i know i said i don't like to go out on
the road, i didn't used to, anyway, but...well, just let
me finish. emma was gone, and we ate dinner...we
may have even ordered out that night; that probably
sounds horrible, but deborah just couldn't stand over
the stove right then, so it seems like we had a pizza...
yeah, one from sbarro's, over at the mall. we had pizza,
deb holding my hand under the table the whole time,
all through the silence...and we went to bed right after.
(beat) the phone woke me about eleven thirty. i almost
had to pry deborah's fingers off of mine to get it, but
i was on by about the third, maybe the fourth ring.
it was him. the police detective and very apologetic
about calling so late, and the whole process and the
usual stuff that you'd see on any of those cop programs
on t v. we don't watch them much—maybe the kids
do, when we're not around, but they're not supposed
to—but you know the kind i mean. he was like that...
(beat) it'd all come out fine, he said, ruled "natural
causes" after a few tests'd been run and he just wanted
to let us know and if there was anything he could do
he'd be glad to...i hung up without him finishing, he'd
put us through enough that day. on a day like that, a
day no parent should ever have to face, and to have
those...people do that...so i hung up. i hung up the
receiver and rolled back over to deborah, i just held her
at first...putting my hand back in place and squeezing
her fingers a bit. but it woke her. she woke up and we
whispered to each other...talking under the sheets like
two schoolchildren, about things we hadn't mentioned
in years! we were under the sheets, just them, because
from that night on, deb and i could never sleep with
blankets on that bed again...that's probably odd, isn't
it? maybe not...but we couldn't. middle of winter,
kids'll all be off at ski trips and deborah and me just
huddle together under the sheets, to this day... *(beat)*
anyhow, the talking must've gone on for hours, a few

at least and then the kissing and finally...well, you're
not that drunk, you don't need to hear it all. we did
what you'd imagine you might do on a night like
that, a moment when your entire universe has been
changed forever. *(beat)* i don't know, but that may have
even been the night that joe was...that's our youngest,
"Joseph" yes, and i have a brother of the same name,
so...but joe came almost exactly nine months later,
he's a great boy, he really is. and over time, and with
the new child...life goes on. it does, and it's strange to
say that, you know, because i'd never believe it from
hearing some other person say it, i mean, if i heard that
i'd just never buy it, because of the loss, and you know,
i'd feel everybody was just smiling and pretending to
be all understanding, but they really think that you're
like some chinese family getting rid of the daughter
to get a son and just crazy things'd run through my
head... but then it happens to you, and it's true. *(beat)*
you just go on. you do. you thank your heavenly father
for giving you strength to stand up to his trials and
figure there must be a plan behind it all, a reason for so
much pain and you just...go on.

(pause)

and that's what we did. we went on...and more than
that. a lot more... *(beat)* lemme fill your glass there
or you're not gonna...well, okay. if you're fine, then
you're fine. umm... *(beat)* so...so, so, so.

(pause)

i've gotten off the path here...somehow. *(checks watch)*
umm, look at the...you're sure you've got the time for
this? *(beat)* well, there's not much left to tell, anyhow,
so finish off that drink and i'll be done...i promise.

(pause)

alright, umm...there was a problem. that's what had
started all this, i mean, originally, started it all in

motion...a problem at work. we'd been taken over
recently, i mean, no big deal in theory, happened all
the time during the 80s, somebody else takes over, you
lose a few of the stragglers, guys who couldn't keep
up...and i do mean "guys" as in everybody, all people
here, because it was usually women at that point,
not always, but a lot of the time...takeovers were an
excellent way to get things back in order, and that's
not just me talking, you know...there's definitely an
order to things in business, and the old boys at the
top, the guys you never even see, just their pictures in
the hallway...they like things the way they've always
been. so that's when a bunch of these women with
their m.b.a.s and affirmative action nonsense would
get the boot. nothing personal about it, at least i never
felt there was...just getting everything spinning back
the way it was supposed to be. *(beat)* but not this time.
no, this time it was gonna happen, and nobody could
tell which way things would end up. everybody at
my level; that mid-management level of things...was
pretty vulnerable and it came down that we could
count on four of us from the salt lake office being let
go—that's where i worked, commuted in from orem
every day because of the standard of living that area
afforded us—and it'd just be up to fate as to who
got the axe. another cliché, right? yeah, well, i'm full
of `em. or it, full of it, one of the two...can't be sure
anymore. *(beat)* so, that was the story, four of us were
going to go, three of which i and everyone else had
a pretty good idea of, three that should've gone a
long time ago, but that last spot...that was the one.
the tough call. there was me, who'd been steady and
strong and average, you know, just average or slightly
above, someone that they could count on, good sense
of humor and everything for the past seven years, well
liked and i liked everyone. or, most everyone, there
was this woman, a few years younger than me and had

come in during a wave of new hires about four years
back...just plain vicious, i mean, talk about clichés and
all that, she was a walking one...the business suit and
blunt cut hair thing going, can't remember ever even
seeing her smile, you know what i'm saying... but
she knew her stuff, i knew it, we all did, and so did
she and she reveled in it. the sales, the numbers, the
whole game. we'd gotten off badly...actually, i'd made
a mistake once, a board meeting where i'd grouped
her in with a "you guys oughta..." meaning that side
of the table and she called me out on it...first meeting,
or maybe the second, she'd been to and she nails me
out loud about my attitude, my limited "chauvinist
lexicon" and all this other, just, crap that she fired off.
walked out of the room in silence and me and some of
the other guys laughed it off over lunch, but i caught
one or two of the other women smiling to themselves
as the meeting broke up. just this slight thing, but i
caught it...anyway, i always felt one step behind her
after that, like she made it her job to one up me from
that moment on... *(beat)* but she was one. me, and
her, because of the short time she'd been there, and a
couple other folks that had about the same seniority
that i did...and that's what hung over our heads,
each of us, day after day as we'd go into work. it was
coming, we knew that, it was going to happen and
all we could do was look at each other as we sat there
waiting...

(pause)

i got the call just before deb had gone to safeway. took
it in the den because it was coming from chicago...a
friend of mine, at the home office, a guy from school
actually, with a tip. a tip he'd heard that day and
wanted to call me with it...it was me. i was the one that
would make up the four, and he was so sorry and all
that—he's a really good guy, i see him whenever i'm

in chicago, we were these really big jokers when we
were at school, in the dorms together and so he was
just doing what any guy would do, he said, letting
me hear it from a friendly voice, and giving me a
jump, the weekend, anyway, before he hung up he
said again it was just what was going around, but he
thought i should know… *(beat)* i couldn't even look at
deb as she was going out to the van. she called out to
me, told me to crawl in and get a little snooze before
the kids got home and they'd be right back…but i just
waved to her. couldn't look, you know, not right then,
just waved my hand, i was too busy looking around
the house, at our things, i mean, all the things we'd
gathered in ten years together, and at the house itself
and, well, just all of it…what was i gonna do? how
could i possibly keep it all going, the lifestyle we'd
made for ourselves, without my seniority, the benefit
package…jobs all over being tight like they are? it just
wouldn't be possible… *(beat)* it was like the moment in
that film *kramer vs kramer*, you know, where he decides
he's got to get a job that day, right? i felt like that…i
keep bringing up movies and t v and i don't mean to,
because we really don't watch all that much, but there
is some good programming out there, and that was an
especially moving one, i thought, the way he fought
that battle with his wife over the child and…but i'm
standing there, just taking in the v c r, and our big
screen t v and one of the kid's bikes, i can see through
the front window, the pathfinder, *wheel of fortune*'s
blasting on the t v. in the family room…all these
thoughts are swirling around in my head. and i hear
it. *(beat)* i wasn't asleep…i couldn't of been, i mean,
i've tried to believe it, make myself believe it, too, but i
wasn't, or i never would've heard her. the baby, emma,
in the other room. as i was standing there i heard her
cry out from inside the bedroom. i did… *(beat)* when i
got to the doorway she was already under the blankets,

she was, i swear, under them and fighting to get out.
it's just reflexes, i guess, because she wasn't big enough
to do anything about it, i mean, she'd just started to
crawl a few weeks before that, and she was tiny for her
age, the doctors said that...but she'd managed to get
herself down under that comforter, i rushed in there,
to the edge of the carpet at the bedroom door and then,
i don't know, something stopped me. just stopped me
like some invisible force had reached out and took
hold of the back of my shirt and yanked me to a halt...i
looked in at her again, this little yelp kind of coming up
from her as she blundered around in there...it almost
looked like when your puppy, as a kid, or the family
cat, you know, would get put under the blankets for
a laugh, it was like that, almost. this little...mound...
wandering around in there, it was nearly absurd, to
walk in on something like this, i mean, you just could
never be ready for a thing like that, and because of
that, that specific part of it, the unreality...i was able
to make the decision, in that moment, standing there
watching my daughter fight for her life, i made my
decision, this is very hard to...anyway, remember
i said i hated to waste things? well, when i looked
at it, i mean, rationally, for even half-a-second there
in the hallway, i realized that's what this was. an
opportunity, and i wasn't going to waste it... *(beat)* so
i—i'm just gonna say this, because it's a little...so, i
went into the room and stood there by the bed, i stood
there and pulled up the comforter by one corner and i
saw her then. her little fine sandy hair and her...i just
kind of coaxed her down a bit. down a bit further with
the edge of my foot, turned her a touch and down and
then i dropped the covers back and walked out...there
was one last little sound emma made, you could barely
hear it. but i just kept walking, back out to the loveseat,
there in the family room, and layed down and made
myself go to sleep, put a pillow over my head so i

couldn't hear…and drifted off. *(beat)* the point i wanna make, though, see, is that it didn't have to happen that way. i took the risk, this calculated risk for my family that this whole episode would play out in our favor, give me that little edge at work and maybe things'd be okay, or they'd change their minds because of, you know…but it didn't have to be like that. if deb had just hurried a bit, if she hadn't stop to look through *people* magazine or her mother hadn't gone next door to fill a prescription, then who knows? maybe they would've got back in time and emma would still be…that sounds strange, doesn't it, that way of thinking? but all i'm saying is, it was fate that took her, just the whimsy of a lingering red light or a prolonged chat with one of our neighbors in the produce aisle or if i hadn't heard her cry out in the first place, i mean, i could've gotten into bed there beside her, i was planning to, i might've fallen asleep and never even heard her. then…who knows? it probably would've happened anyway, and it did happen, and so you go on. like i said before, you just go on…

(pause)

i kept my job. i did. and guess who was the one, i mean, after all that, guess who got it right between the eyes? another cliché, i know, but boy oh boy, what a great one it was… *(beat)* i even walked her to the elevator the day she left, her and the other three, this was several months after all the other…i was right behind them with a "so long" and "we'll miss you" and right then, it came to me, it came to me with my friends standing around and that little…well, she wasn't looking so strong anymore, there in the open car, this box of stuff in her hands, as the doors were closing i said to them all, but staring straight at her, i said, "you guys take care now!" just like that, and then they slid shut. huh…just like in *kramer* at the end. the

doors did... *(gestures)* isn't that funny? i never thought
of that before...i said that and we laughed all through
lunch about it, the guys and me.

(pause)

i was at a seminar, big yearly thing the company
put on. this one was in boston, six months back. my
friend from chicago flew in for it. okay, so... after the
morning session, just in passing as we were both in the
restroom at one point, he said something to me, my
friend, i guess trying to lighten things up a little, he
mentioned work. and about the layoffs, and how glad
i must've finally been to have gotten rid of you know
who. and then he said, "boy, i really had you going
that friday, didn't i?" i turned to him, standing there
at the urinal, my fly still open and i turned to him and
the whole picture was clear to me. right then, it was as
clear as a look into the future...what he'd done. what
we always used to do to each other, see, he'd heard the
real truth about what was coming and just couldn't
let it go without a little razzing and so he'd given me
the call, let me stew about it over that weekend...he
was going to buzz me back monday morning with the
truth, but by then... *(beat)* yeah, he'd gotten me, alright,
he got me good, just like the old days.

(pause)

so i travel now, same pay and everything, a little better
actually, but i consult for our regional branches, even
nationally sometimes...and it keeps me going. deb and
i are fine. joe's getting huge, he really is, i'd show you
a picture but i don't have any on me...but i find i really
like the driving these days, you know? gives me a lot of
time to just...well, drive, just drive and think, i usually
don't even get a room; i got this place *(gestures)* because
i'm here a few days but normally, i'd have everything
in the trunk and just do it that way ...it's funny how

things end up, isn't it? *(beat)* i can't tell deb, it'd kill her. kill us, as a family, i mean, that's obvious, right? can't tell anyone in the church, or the police, of course...so i chose you. i saw you, tonight as i was walking through the lobby, and i just chose you. so there it is...i'm finished.

(pause)

you probably need to...yeah, it's late. take care of yourself, and thanks again, seriously, you've been very...you have any kids? no? well, when you do, you be good to them, okay? there's nothing like `em in the world...believe me. *(beat)* why don't you go ahead and shut the light off there on your way out, if you would...i'm just gonna sit here a bit. i'll be fine. you go ahead, really, it's almost time for the last call, so you should...i'll be...fine, i will. *(after a moment)* goodnight...

(he smiles weakly once and takes a last sip from his glass as the lights snap off.)

(silence, darkness)

END OF PLAY

a gaggle of saints

(silence, darkness)

(A young, attractive couple sitting apart from one another, they are dressed in the popular evening fashion of the day.)

JOHN: so, okay, so there was this big bash...

SUE: a party...

JOHN: party, bash, whatever, in the city. that's what we came down for. the thing, this get-together. 's why we did it in the first place...

SUE: 's our old youth group. i got a flyer in the mail...

JOHN: couple churches together, i think, mixed, and meeting in the city. ballroom over at the plaza...

SUE: which really sounded nice, you know...

JOHN: 's expensive.

SUE: i mean, elegant...

JOHN: but that's cool, manhattan, always have a good time there, right?

SUE: people from high school were going...

JOHN: 'cause we're juniors up at b.c., so, like, there's still lots of guys we know...

SUE: seniors now, mostly...

JOHN: all these seniors, guys like that, who we're still in touch with. friends, you know...

SUE: this was just after mid-terms...

JOHN: sue's a year ahead, almost, two semesters, we're juniors, but nearly a year... *(beat)* both going to b.c....

SUE: boston college, you know, we almost didn't get in. i mean, both of us...

JOHN: my g p a, but we'd decided, i mean, early—like back at greeley, junior year, maybe—that we'd do college together.

SUE: and boston seemed about right, you know, four hours from home...

JOHN: 's a little over three, if you push it. i don't like to go crazy with my v w, but it's only about three hours if you're really moving, three, three and a half...

SUE: it's beautiful up around there, i mean, massachusetts. new england, all that's just gorgeous this time of year. leaves turning...

JOHN: it just sounded really great, weekend back in new york. stop in, maybe, say "hi" to the folks...be good to go down for a couple days.

SUE: so i contacted the three people going to school with us...you know, from home, three friends going to b c as well...

JOHN: one guy's even in my house, david's his name ... didn't really hang out with him at home or anything, different, he does gymnastics, but he's cool...

SUE: he's nice. nice guy...

JOHN: ended up, we talked two other couples into going back with us...guy from the house, this david guy.

SUE: we took his car down...

JOHN: ...and a friend of mine, tim, year behind me, but studying at b c, same time...

SUE: 's a beautiful red truck he had. (pause) jeep or something...

JOHN: `cause i've got this old v w, i said that, right? it's great, '73, with the metal bumpers and all that...but needs a tune-up and i'm not gonna drive three hours with all these guys...

SUE: we all thought we could go down together, one car. everybody wanted to, gonna be in the city at this hotel, live band and everything...

JOHN: and so six of us, a girl that's going out with this david from my fraternity, karen's her name, i think... she was coming too. she knew the city pretty well, grew up just off the park and they were getting along good...so it's six altogether now, six for the ride and the v-dub's definitely out of the question.

SUE: david said he'd drive if we wanted.

JOHN: 's got one of those isuzu troopers, 's roomy. big.

SUE: and we're all picked up at three in the afternoon, saturday.

JOHN: it was greek week, well, same weekend as the black and white ball up at school...but we hadn't committed to going, you know, so then sue gets the flyer and suddenly, i'm rushing around, fighting for tuxedos, ten minutes to six, friday afternoon! *(beat)* i ended up buying a perry ellis, finally. a size big, but i got one...looks okay, doesn't it?

SUE: it looked good on him...i had to put a safety pin in the vest, in the back of it, but it was really nice when he had it on...

JOHN: we left 'em in the bags, the three of us guys, hanging in the trooper for the ride. i mean, no sense getting 'em messed up for no reason, right?

SUE: i had this dress i'd been saving...all taffeta, i'd been saving it for something like this...did i mention that? *(beat)* i needed to find some shoes, but i thought the dress was perfect...

JOHN: we missed the game, b c's first conference—'s away, but we could've watched it at our place with a bunch of guys, they always order in pizza and everything—but we said "no", jump in with all these people...road trip.

SUE: tim's girlfriend, patrice, i've known for years...

JOHN: with about a dozen overnight bags, tuxedos hanging from all corners of dave's isuzu... *(beat)* the girls decided to wear their outfits...

SUE: it was my black dress.

JOHN: sue's got this knockout thing, kind of a cutaway in the front, what's it called?

SUE: ...with a scalloped neckline...

JOHN: "scalloped", i think...in the front, you know, over her chest and no back to it at all, not any sleeves, just very little on top. but chic, too, right? classic lines, see, it's a dinner dress, dress you'd wear out to dinner, dining, not something a girl would pick out, junior prom, with spaghetti straps all clotting it up... *(beat)* she looked great, proud to be with her...

SUE: i knew it'd get wrinkled, a little...i did. taffeta's terrible for that, but i thought it sounded wonderful, you know, getting out at some amoco, middle of connecticut, in this wave of taffeta...and buying, i don't know, a milky way, a can of soda. and the attendant's mouth just hanging open at the sight of us...

JOHN: i'm putting gas in, one time we stopped, and look up...i see nothing but chiffon and silk and what-not, miles of it, going down the snack aisle, that killed me!...

SUE: i was carrying my shoes—i did find a pair, even had time to dye them to match—but i took 'em off in the car, and i was just holding them in the store. so, i'm standing there, in my stockings, carrying these shoes...

JOHN: i'll always remember that. her smiling at me, through the glass there, little bit of chocolate on her lips...and carrying her shoes.

SUE: this was going to be a great party... *(pause)* ...i could feel it.

JOHN: the church usually threw a pretty good bash, i mean, times we'd go into the city.

SUE: it was our anniversary...

JOHN: last minute, got her a corsage, not the wrist kind, hate those...but this was beautiful, white blossoms. don't know what kind, but they were white, i remember that...

SUE: i loved it! the softest pink, it was...john thought it was white, but it was really just the lightest shade of pink. the last shade of pink it could be, before turning into something else... *(beat)* and you know? he pricked his finger, john did. as he pinned it on me, pricked his index finger...

JOHN: stupid pin!...

SUE: and then...a spot of blood, just a drop, but he ended up with this touch of blood on his shirt...

JOHN: couldn't even see it if i buttoned the jacket...

SUE: but see, in a weird way, though, it excited me. the blood, is that stupid to say? ...probably, but it did. *(beat)* i mean, it was stunning to look at, you know? all that white on him, the bright of his shirt...and then this splash of...

JOHN: red...

SUE: ...blood on his chest.

JOHN: didn't get any on her dress, however, nothing, felt good about that...wouldn't want to ruin her anniversary dress.

SUE: four years…

JOHN: huh? believe that? four…since fall of our third year in high school, wow…

SUE: i saw him on the track one day. lived six blocks away all my life, in history together, but i never really saw him until he was jogging one time…

JOHN: i like to keep in shape…

SUE: he'd always kept his hair short, trimmed up…

JOHN: my dad cut it. believe that?! sixteen years old and my father drags me into the kitchen, every other sunday. i could just count on the standard "sears portrait" cut. *(beat)* i was always a little worried about my ears. stick out a bit…

SUE: but i see him running, really running, blistering by people who are just jogging or walking and i don't know this guy. 's cute. nice body. and i don't know him… *(beat)* kind of long hair…

JOHN: my dad was away on sabattical in London or some type of thing…i didn't really know or care. i could let my hair grow, that's what i saw coming out of the whole deal, my mom didn't mind at all…

SUE: so i put down my pom poms, and my purse and all that, and i start running, too. i mean, i can't keep up with him but i go a little slower or a little faster every so often so that he's catching me more quickly on every lap.

JOHN: i knew who she was. she was dating a guy i knew…

SUE: that was over. we broke up, like, two weeks before. he was this, i don't know, he'd kind of left the church, and there's this completely bad scene at a party, the screaming, and he's sort 'a drunk, and so

it's over. i mean, we're still calling each other but it's
definitely over...

JOHN: i'd heard this. i mean, you hear everything at
some time in your life, right, and this was a thing you
keep up on in high school, girls you secretly like but
can't get at 'cause they're dating somebody, maybe a
friend, and so you file 'em away and hope the guy joins
the army or gets sent to laos or something...held back
in school, even, and you and she end up on the same
floor, some dorm in florida. *(beat)* the best would be,
like, a major football moment, touchdown to take the
state championship, something majestic like that, but
anything...camp counselors even, would do. she was
that kind of girl...

SUE: and we're running together now, he's pretending
he's winded and needs to slow down and i'm just
trying to keep up and around we go. sun going down,
we're not speaking at all, and we just keep going in
circles...

JOHN: then he shows up...

SUE: we really had stopped dating, but he was going
to give me a ride home, just friendly, because the track
and the practice fields and everything are, like, three
miles from my house...

JOHN: he pulls his car right on the track, into the lanes.
nice new scirroco, all black, that he got as a graduation
gift from his dad. he was a year or so older...

SUE: i slowed down a little.

JOHN: and i can see what's coming because i know
him and we've had some laughs together, not friends,
exactly, but friends of friends, that's what we are...

SUE: but i don't want to leave.

JOHN: this is how we first got together, it's kind of a
funny story...

SUE: so he chases me down on the track, because we just jog by him, right around his car for a couple laps, and keep going...

JOHN: why am i gonna stop? he's not my boyfriend...

SUE: we weren't really dating, you couldn't call it that, anymore...

JOHN: see, and he grabs me. turns me around, after grabbing me, he turns me and says, "hey!" and he's holding onto me, about my size, and one of his nails is digging into my nipple, holding my chest like he is. he's got these, like, long nails on one hand...

SUE: he plays guitar, he's very good...

JOHN: and this hurts and i'm standing there thinking, "this doesn't need to be happening..." and i turn on him. never spoke to him the whole time, just turned on him and flipped him over onto the ground and started pounding on his head. it's a surface track so he's not getting too banged up but i'm hitting him pretty good and sue's just standing there...waiting.

SUE: i'd never seen this happen before...

JOHN: finally he stops squirming around and i hit him one more time, you know high schoolers, right, you go a bit overboard in a fight, and then i walk over and grab her stuff and give it to her and we take off. scirroco's still sitting there, people having to jog around it, sun dancing off the hood of the thing as we head home.

SUE: we walked all the way...

JOHN: noticed my reflection in it as we go by. bloody nose, him grabbing at me...

SUE: ...i had, like, two huge blisters the next day.

JOHN: and i kissed her, standing there on her porch, still didn't say anything but we've been dating four

years since then and never heard back from the other
guy after that. *(beat)* i shot baskets with him about a
year ago, over at the elementary, and he didn't seem so
mad...

SUE: sometimes we fight, we do, like anybody else, or
break up...whatever, john dated someone for a week
or so, freshman year, i met this guy in a biology class.
didn't last... *(beat)* we're getting engaged this summer,
we already planned it...

JOHN: point being, it's our anniversary, right, and we're
hoping for this great time and whatnot, want it all to be
special, weekend in the city, girls wanna go shopping
in "the village" if there's time, whatever... *(beat)* we
talked about taking the train on the way back, alone.
sleeping car... *(pause)* ...i'm kidding. they don't even
have those.

SUE: mid-terms last week everybody just needed to get
away.

JOHN: ends up we do go to my parent's house on
sunday...dad makes me sit down, "you look like a
bushman", first thing out of his mouth—what's he
mean by that?—and he tries to give me a haircut!
halfway through my pre-med, he's still trying to cut
my bangs!

SUE: i thought it was kind of funny...i could hear them
arguing in the other room. his hair really does look
better when it's long. it does...

JOHN: but that's later, anyway...

SUE: so we make it to the city in, like, less than four
hours, weekend traffic, that's not bad.

JOHN: does it look stupid? seriously...no, i mean it. are
my ears funny at all?

SUE: eighteen-fifty for ten hours parking, that's a lot, i
thought...and then we all walk over to the hotel, the

guys carrying these big dry cleaning bags over their shoulders...

JOHN: we decided to go in on a room, all of us...not for anything, i mean, you know. i'm just telling you, so we could change and everything. better than wrinkling our stuff up. right?

SUE: we get in, still a few hours before the party's going to start, so we all decide to use the facilities, you know, take a jacuzzi, whatever, lots of time to get changed again...'s fun. *(beat)* i got back into my dress...

JOHN: i'm tying up my shoes, lacing 'em up...she comes out of the bathroom, like i said, this is four years we've been going together and i'm still staring at the best-looking girl i've ever seen. i'm just completely in love. serious...

SUE: makeup, try and put make up on in some hotel bathroom and you'll understand the meaning of devotion, sinks in those places, even the plaza, are impossibly small, postage stamp of a mirror i'm using...but i want to took nice for him. *(beat)* i bought a new lipstick in the lobby. they had a counter there...'s vivid, crimson...

JOHN: she steps into the living room of this hotel suite, city full of models and actresses...the beautiful people...and i can't see anything else. 's like we're thrown back to the garden, the two of us, watching one another across this great green meadow, my side still hurting from the missing rib and all, but she's revealed to me, golden hair and a face like fresh snow and i'm thinking...hey, screw the bone, you know, here's why he rested on the seventh day. 'cause they can't get any better than this. *(beat)* i mean, i'm not so poetic or whatever, but this is exactly what i'm thinking.

SUE: the dress helps a lot, because i'm not going to kid myself, it does, but i can see he's happy, and his tux

looks really handsome, it was going to be great, a really
good evening, i could feel it...

JOHN: and we walk downstairs, arm in arm. man, feels
so nice to stroll past all these people, i mean, rich guys,
girl like that on my arm! made me feel strong, you
know? powerful...the crowd almost glides apart as we
approach.

SUE: we've got nowhere to go. the party's not until
later...nothing but possibilities...wherever we looked, i
really felt that, walking along.

JOHN: so on and on...couple hours pass, david's girlfriend, "karen", takes the lead at some point, walking
us through the park...over by that one bridge, the big
pond? by the delacorte, moon's smiling down and all,
romance hanging over a night like this out of some
storybook, some tale by, maybe, scott fitzgerald or
those guys...i really do love this girl. that's the thing
that's screaming out in my head right then...

SUE: he was holding my hand so tight...

JOHN: there's a swan or two out on the water, little
breeze, october, but still warm, you know how that
can be...perfect, a perfect night, and then, just off to
our left, there's this, like, patch of woods near the path.
comes this rustling...

SUE: i thought it might be some teenagers or who
knows what. we all started to walk a bit faster....

JOHN: i'm not scared but it's night, city all around...
what else can you do, girls with you? so we walk
along. *(beat)* and two guys, middle-aged guys, l l bean
shirts on and the whole thing...come out of the dark.
smiling, and i don't need a map to tell me what's been
going on... *(pause)* ...i don't.

SUE: it was just two men. walking along...no big deal.

JOHN: coming out of the weeds, they were, off in the park alone, and these smiles, i don't know, i just don't know what to think about it. i mean, we're going to this party, all dressed up, what should we care, right? one dude looks like my father, a little, it's dark but he had that look, right, that settled, satisfied sort of... anyway, off they head, arms linked together and nothing we say ever going to change what they are... *(pause)* dance all night, sue as stunning as she's ever looked and i'm telling you, i can't get that picture, the image of it, out of my head. those smiles, i can't do it... *(beat)* but the party is great, it really is...

SUE: i haven't danced like that in a long time...

JOHN: it was, like, the beginning of a magical evening ...everything was right, it was pristine, you know? soothing, and we just kept dancing, the two of us. danced for hours...round and round.

SUE: they'd done the whole place, the room, i mean, when we finally got inside...in blues, and golds, with these great moons, these golden crescents hanging above us...

JOHN: like smiles, like the moon smiling down...

SUE: i think we looked pretty nice together, looked like a couple, you know?

JOHN: it was fun, back like that, in the city...'s always fun. saw a lot of guys we know...

SUE: my little sister was there...there with some boy from greeley, he's in debate, he said. seemed nice enough...she likes him.

JOHN: we ran into sue's sister, did she mention that?

SUE: hadn't seen her since august...

JOHN: younger sister, maureen, with some kid...

SUE: he's been drinking.

JOHN: ahh, he was okay. *(beat)* had a good band going. reggae...

SUE: i'd never been to the plaza before, i mean, past it, shopping and whatever, with my mom, but never to it. it was tremendous! so much glass. high white walls, it was like...a cake, some wedding cake, left on the corner there, downtown. 's what it reminded me of... *(beat)* the whole thing, though...the trip, dance and all...made me sleepy.

JOHN: sue went upstairs to our room, room we'd rented, with karen and tim's girlfriend...patrice...

SUE: i'd known patrice since kindergarden...

JOHN: said they wanted to take a quick nap, just a half-hour, whatever, then we'd go get a bite. this was, like, maybe, one-thirty...

SUE: 's a king-size bed. a gold comforter on it...

JOHN: so, we hung out downstairs a bit, talked to some guys from home...david, tim, and me.

SUE: we all fell asleep, together on that bed...

JOHN: i was a touch bored, you know, room was warm, and lots of people we didn't recognize...so i suggested a walk. "let's head over to the park." about six, seven guys all together, it was still nice out...

SUE: i'm not sure what time it was...

JOHN: we strolled around a bit, over by the paris theater, some guy, younger guy, kicked over a garbage can...i mean, it happens. you get together, doing stuff, no big deal. 's just garbage... *(pause)* fifteen, twenty minutes later we split up, lot of the high schoolers want to get back to the bash, but us three, tim, david, and me...no hurry, we just kind 'a wander around, hanging out. after a while, we shoot over into central park, the 59th street entrance...looking around, talking.

's really dark in there. only lights coming from the
buildings, way off. kind of exciting…

SUE: i thought i looked up at two, or two-fifteen…but
i'm not sure. 'cause i kept sleeping…

JOHN: …and then i saw 'em. both of them. those guys…

SUE: i was so tired…

JOHN: they were saying "goodnight…" well, not saying
it exactly, but kissing, two men, grown men, standing in this park, public park in the middle of new york
and kissing like something out of a clark gable film.
tongues out, and the arms around each other, and
nothing else in the world matters to these two…just
finishing off the date, big night at the symphony, or
some foreign film, who knows? but it's this "see you
soon" and "thanks so much" and hands all where they
shouldn't be. i mean, come on, i know the scriptures,
know 'em pretty well, and this is wrong. *(beat)* we all
kind 'a squeeze up against a couple trees, off in the
shadows, tim crouching on the ground, watching this.
out near "the ramble". oh man…man! you know, you
read about it, or even see that film, what is it, with the
"superman" guy? *deathtrap*, right, and you live with
it. don't love it, don't condone it for the world, still,
you go on living, live and let live, whatever, but this,
i figure, is flaunting it. i mean, as much our park as
theirs, and we're in town one night, that's all, one…
and we got 'a witness this? *(pause)* men old enough to
be our fathers—i mean, middle-aged, and clutching at
one another like romeo and juliet! *(beat)* they whisper
something, and chuckle for a second, hand on each
others bottoms…i start to feel sick, i mean it, nauseous.
then a last peck on the cheek and one disappears down
a trail, headed for the west side. he's gone. the other
glances around, taking in the night, i guess, big smile
up at the moon…and he kind of casually strolls over

to this "men's room". fifty yards off. concrete building,
with the steps down into it. whistling while he goes...
he was whistling. i don't even stop to think this
through, but motion the guys to follow me.

SUE: i thought about getting out of my dress, but
i couldn't move. all of us, we were sleeping so
peacefully... *(beat)* did you know patrice snores? she
does...a little.

JOHN: as we're moving down the landing into the
restroom, i glance at tim...'s got that look. recognize
that look anywhere, and he's starting to smile...

SUE: i don't think i even dreamed that night...

JOHN: before going in i told the guys to hold off, wait
out here for me 'til they got my signal...and that's the
plan. wait for me to flush him out, make sure no one
wanders by. when i get inside, 's like another world...
walls are exploding with graffiti, place stinks, two
bulbs burnt out. some old dude curled up, asleep in a
corner, and our friend's legs, i spot, patiently sitting in
a stall, waiting, and not a care in this world, i slip into
the booth next to his, start fumbling with my belt, this,
that, and like clockwork, this guy's hand comes up
under my side of the partition, his signal, pink fingers,
wiggling up at me. imploring. i notice this thin gold
band on his little finger, catching the light. *(beat)* so, i
lay my open palm in his and two minutes later we're
standing near the mirrors—big pieces of stainless steel,
really—standing, and sizing each other up. small talk.
name's "chet", he says, and i don't even bat an eyelash
as he moves in, his lips playing across my cheek, let
his tongue run along my teeth and a hand, free hand,
tracing down my fly...i just smile at him, smile and
even lick his chin for a second, for a single second, i see
his shoulders relax. then i whistle, i let out a whistle
that sends him stumbling back, blinking, and kind of

waving his hands in the air as tim and dave appear in
the doorway, he looks at them, looks and comes back
from his fantasies long enough to touch down on earth,
a flicker in his eyes, realizing no good can come from
this...and starts babbling, this guy, "chet", probably
a v p some bank on park avenue, and he's babbling
and wetting himself like an infant, i don't remember
exactly, but i think he even got on his knees, down on
his knees and the pleading, begging. *(beat)* my first shot
catches him against the cheek, just under the eye and
he slams into a sink. all snot and blood running down.
with so many of us hitting, tearing at him, it's hard to
get off a clean punch but i know i connect a few more
times, i feel his head, the back of it, softening as we go,
but i just find a new spot and move on. tim kicking him
long after he's blacked out... *(pause)* finally, we start
to relax a bit, looking at what we've done. exhausted,
spent, i mean, this man is not moving, may never move
again and we know it's time to leave, believe this, guy
in the corner, sleeps through it all?! *(beat)* before we
go, tim leans into it one more time, takes a little run at
it, smashing his foot against the bridge of this man's
nose and i see it give way. just pick up and move to the
other side of his face. wow. and then it's silence, not a
sound, and for the first time, we look over at dave. tim
and me. i mean, really look at him. us together, tim,
myself, that's one thing, it's unspoken, our bond, but
we don't know david. don't really know him...what's
he thinking? and right then, as if to answer us through
revelation...he grabs up the nearest trash can, big wire
mesh thing, raises it above his head as he whispers,
"fag". i'll never forget that..."fag". that's all. and brings
that can down right on the spine of the guy, who just
sort of shudders a bit, expelling some air. boom! right
on his back, as i'm leaning down, pulling that ring off
his pinkie. *(beat)* i told you i noticed it... *(pause)* then,
and i still can't even believe this, then tim does the

most amazing thing, this'll go down, the record books, there, with the three of us over this guy's body, he starts offering up a short eulogy, i mean, i'm getting delirious, this is, like, almost surreal…and halfway through, tim's praying along, we all start giggling, like schoolboys, we're howling, tears running down, can't catch our breath we find it all so funny! and that's how we leave him… *(beat)* slip out, one by one, running back toward the plaza in the dark and whooping it up like indians, war cries, and running with just a trace of moonlight dancing off the pond as we go…

SUE: the phone woke me up…

JOHN: we called the room from the street, wanted to take the girls out to breakfast, say they'll be down in fifteen minutes… *(pause)* we waited outside.

SUE: i got the other girls up…took a minute, but i got them up. i felt really refreshed… *(pause)* …i did.

JOHN: dave's walking around on the curb, talking to himself, and tim pulls me aside, asks me, wants to know one thing. "what?" i say. wants to know why i touched the guy. let him kiss me. see, he'd seen it happen, glanced inside, and seen it. *(beat)* but i didn't know, didn't have an answer, isn't that strange?

SUE: it was so quiet in the lobby as we were leaving. i started tip-toeing out. isn't that funny?

JOHN: i couldn't answer him, and you know, he never asked me again, he didn't. *(beat)* he pointed out to me, though, that my shirt had blood on it, a misting of blood, probably off the guy as i was getting the ring. my tux was covered, so, got 'a think quick, i asked tim to hit me in the face, give me a bloody nose so i could explain it to sue. *(beat)* only hurt for a second…

SUE: we all met in front of the hotel, and i saw john's face. aaah! all cut up like it was…see, he'd fallen down,

racing along the fountain out front, balancing on it, and
slipped, scraped himself up and blood on everything.
(beat) silly games...

JOHN: had a great meal...you know, you can't get
those german sausages for breakfast, the big fat ones,
anywhere but manhattan, you can't...

SUE: i was eating my french toast, just eating along
and i notice this glint in my water glass, a spark of
light. *(beat)* john'd slipped a ring in it! a beautiful gold
thing...i loved him so much at that moment.

JOHN: "happy anniversary", i said...

SUE: it was a little big, but fit pretty well. had this wonderful leaf pattern, all the way around...

JOHN: looked nice on her. i liked it...

SUE: i kissed him there, in front of everybody, and he
blushed a bit. we all laughed, i can't tell you what a
wonderful weekend we had...

JOHN: we did end up taking the amtrak back up...just
sue and myself, dave dropped us at grand central and,
you know, lots of "thank you" and "see you monday!"
(beat) tim even gave me a hug. first time he's even done
that...

SUE: it was my idea...the train.

JOHN: and we saw our parents, stopped in sunday and
even made it to church...that was really nice.

SUE: i like relief sunday school at home so much
better...

JOHN: had dinner with the folks, then the late train up
to boston.

SUE: you know, on the way back—it's funny, i
shouldn't even bring this up—a fight broke out. well,
not really a fight but this argument between a man and
his girlfriend, a lot of yelling, she stands up, and starts

pulling on her coat and this guy, i mean, middle of a crowded compartment, just backhands her. he did...

JOHN: knocked her up against the window, really hard...

SUE: everybody got quiet, i could feel john tense up, getting all tense, but the couple was, i don't know, kind of dirty-looking and they seemed like, you know, those kind of people—i don't know what i mean by that, exactly, but they were—so i asked john, whispered to him, to "let it go". *(beat)* and you know what? he didn't so much as bat an eyelash. just kept holding my hand. holding it and playing with the ring on my finger, that made me so happy...

JOHN: i could see he'd given her a bloody nose...

SUE: and they pretty much quieted down right after that. 's no big deal...

JOHN: anyway...

SUE: anyway, we are getting engaged this summer, for sure. did i tell you that?

JOHN: and finally, as we tumbled along toward massachusetts, nearly midnight...i could feel sue fall asleep against my shoulder, all warm. protected.

SUE: i hope it's a fall wedding, you know? i always think they're the most beautiful...

JOHN: but not me...i couldn't drift off. just couldn't do it. so i sat up, watching the lights dance by, the moon grinning down. and you know, i started whistling to myself, i did...

SUE: i was sleeping. asleep there on john's arm, but i'd swear i could hear music...

JOHN: not loud, i mean, don't even recall the tune. but i was whistling, i was. that much i remember...

SUE: ...this beautiful music as i was sleeping, like the sound of angels calling us home...

(they sit together in silence for a moment, finally, they rise and embrace, waiting for their picture to be taken, they smile broadly.)

(harsh blast of a camera's flashbulb.)

(silence, darkness)

END OF PLAY

medea redux

(silence, darkness)

(WOMAN sits alone in a chair at an institutional-style table. a harsh light hangs down directly overhead.)

(a tape player, water carafe and cup, cigarettes, and an ashtray are close at hand.)

(she finishes a cigarette, stubs it out, and slowly begins to speak.)

WOMAN: ...can i just speak? 's that okay? i mean, i'll talk about, but...i got 'a sort of ease into it, you know? 'cause i was never, like, this major talker or anything... like to keep things to myself, some people'd call it "private" or whatever, but it's more like just being sort 'a "inward". right? i'm an inward kind 'a person...i think it depends a lot on the way you grow up, you know, family and all, and i just ended up more inward than anything...anyway, i found that a lot of times, when you ask for stuff, or, like, have maybe questions to things...there's not always an answer out there, you can ask over and over, but you don't all the time hear something back... *(beat)* speaking 'a that, you can hear me, okay, right? can ya? i guess so...

(she begins to speak, then stops, considers, finally, she begins again, very slowly.)

...it's interesting, you know, how things'll work out. well, not "out", i guess, not so much that as maybe just "through". right? things get worked through...or work themselves through. we probably don't have all that much to do with it. we like to think we do, though,

right? god, like we're in on all the big planetary
decisions and shit, you know? but, uh-uh...you wanna
know what i feel, i think we're just spinning around
out here, completely out 'a whack and no way of ever
getting it right again, i mean, back on track or whatever...just can't do it. see, we been doing things wrong
for so long now that it all starts to feel okay after a
while, you know, like this is how it oughta be. *(beat)*
there's a greek word for that...i learned it in school,
he taught it to me...well, i guess i more like "heard"
it from him, if i'd 'a learned it i could tell you what it
is, right? yeah. i know it's greek, though, i caught that
much, but i don't remember what it was...

(she thinks quietly for a moment.)

no...'s too long ago now. had something to do with
the world, the whole thing, coming off its axis or
something, going off in the wrong direction from how
it's all supposed to be. and it's the fault of people, or
"mortals", that's what my teacher said, "mortals are to
blame." see, he said it was simply the fact that—and i
never could understand this, maybe i just didn't listen
good enough, that was the usual problem—but he said
it all stemmed from just our being mortal, right? *(beat)*
so, then every problem we got is from being mortals
...or humans, that's what "mortals" means...and just
because we are what we are, these "mortals", it's, like,
our fault, explain me that...

(she stops for a moment and lights a cigarette.)

you know, a lot of times i just couldn't make clear what
was coming out 'a his mouth, he was really smart,
though, had, like, two college degrees or something,
and still wanted to work at public school, i kind 'a
admired that. i was in his class, one of 'em, his first
year. 's great...he took us, my class anyway, on a
bunch 'a stuff, field trips, like museums, and up to

chicago one time. that was fun. we went there, maybe
twenty-five or so of us, the school bus, and i remember
we were going along that one road, runs past the lake
up there... god, that was beautiful! he looked back,
my teacher did, sitting up by the driver, and saw
all of us kids smashed up against our windows and
staring out, every one of us with our eyes glued to
that water! so, he had the driver pull off at an exit and
we got, maybe, fifteen minutes or so to run around
on the beach...this was november...chase each other,
throw rocks, whatever, but all i did was stand there,
stand down by the edge of the surf and watch the
waves coming in. there in my little red windbreaker,
and i dunno, i felt like an astronaut. or a kind 'a time
explorer, maybe, some scout or something, sent on
ahead, down to earth to see just what the fuck all the
fuss's about...and taking it all in for the first time. you
know? i still remember that. 's kind 'a like that moment
in that one movie, with all the monkeys and that one
guy, he does those commercials for...*planet of the apes*,
that's the one. it's like that, remember, when he rides
down the beach and realizes that he's home after all,
and there's no going back, and he's screaming and
everything, pounding his fist up at the sky, but he's
still sort 'a caught up in it all, too, like, taken in by the
awesomeness of what he's seen...i mean, it was better
than that, i thought, maybe just because of my age at
the time, it was better, but it reminded me of that a
little, it did...

(she stops, taking an extra long drag on her smoke.)

you know what's funny? he hit on me, my teacher did,
on one of those trips, yeah. not on that one, this was at
the maritime center a couple months later...scared the
shit out 'a me! i didn't even know what he was doing
at first—i mean, okay, i did, but i was, like, thirteen—
and that's just not what you're expecting at that age.

well, maybe it never is…he came up behind me at the
observation tank, right, where they've got the sharks
and everything, see, this other teacher was with us and
she wanted to take the rest of the children on down
the passageway—'cause they have a place where you
can handle different sea things, shells and crabs and
stuff, and the shark tank has this dark room connected
to it so that you can stand there and see without a
glare all over the windows, and some kids were sort 'a
scared—but i was always interested in sharks and all
that, i was. you know, you have to pick a vocation in
seventh grade, they make you do that in junior high,
on this "career day", right? and i chose "marine biolo-
gist". i did. out 'a all the other kinds of things they had
there, i picked that one, 'cause i love the water, always
have…so, my teacher said it'd be okay if i stayed
and watched, we'd catch up later… *(beat)* well, i'm
keeping my eye on this one big hammerhead, that's a
species of shark—you probably knew that—and he's
darting in real close to the glass, this hammerhead
is…suddenly, i feel all this weight up against me. my
teacher is pushing me forward with his body, up onto
the observation windows, and i can't move. he never
said anything while it was happening, i mean, to
me—i could hear him whispering something about the
"tragic nobility of sea creatures", some shit like that—
and all i can see, i can't turn at all, the way he's got me
held there, all i can see is this shark, the one i'd been
watching, coming out of the murk and sweeping past
me, again and again…and it's not 'till he's right on top
of me, and turned each time, that i can see his eye. he
turns past the glass at the last second and his eye just
sort 'a rolls back all white as he passes …fuck, that was
scary, i've never forgotten it. that feeling, his weight
on me, and watching as that hammerhead just kept
circling around… *(beat)* well, what the hell, it's easy to
scare a kid. right?

*(she plays a moment with the butt of her cigarette in the
ashtray.)*

anyway, he wouldn't look at me after that, my teacher,
not even a glance, the whole rest of the trip. and he was
always real nice before, and funny to me...i mean, not
in a bad way, not like inappropriately so, i don't think,
but—no, i wasn't even a "teacher's pet" or whatever—
he was just sort 'a open with me. jokes, and showing
me pictures in magazines, like, after that career thing
he would hang up undersea stuff in class, and bringing
in pieces 'a coral to look at...we were starting to be
friends, i thought, at least sort of friendly, because
it's hard, i think, for a teacher in school, like, junior
high, where nobody cares, kids just wanna do sports,
and dances, hang out with their friends, you know...
so, if you meet a person who is actually interested,
like i was, and i really was—i wasn't the smartest or
remembered the most, like i said, but—i was genuinely
interested in things, i wanted to learn, right, i felt like i
needed to comprehend a little about the universe, you
know? i did. 'cause it intrigues me. the way it works,
yeah. *(beat)* and i think a teacher can pick up on that.
and he just responded to it...so, we started to sort 'a
hang out a bit...just at school, the library, or looking at
slides in the resource center, lunchtimes. *(beat)* it was
good, umm...'s good, that's all. i mean, fuck, i was
thirteen, okay, it was nice to have somebody look at
you and not say to pick up your socks...something like
that. let's face it, thirteen's a pretty shitty age, right?

(pause)

but he wouldn't look over at me after that...

(she stops a moment.)

he did give me a ride home, though, from school. he
did do that. i mean, nothing, not a look on the outing,
sits way away from me on the bus, but back at our

building, see, he's responsible for us, and all the
parents are there, this is a friday, and my dad doesn't
show. he doesn't show up. we go into the office, call his
work, nothing at home, and he doesn't come. half-hour
goes by, nobody at school but us. sitting there on the
curb, waiting for my dad. finally he says, my teacher,
he can drop me if i want. he drove this late model
peugeot—i remember 'cause i once asked him to teach
me how to say it—kind of a cream color peugeot, and
he said he'd run me home if i'd like that. 's what he
said, "if you'd like that". *(beat)* in the car, like this was
yesterday, i recall he had this woman singing on the
tape player, real soft and painful, i remember, 'cause i
had to ask who this was. i mean, this was not the bee
gees and i'd never heard anything like it. so fragile-
sounding, you know? he said it was "billie holiday",
that was her name, and it was all he ever played. first
thing he'd said to me, i mean, practically, in five hours
is "billie holiday". and he smiled, it was dark out, but
i could see him smiling there, we're sitting at a light,
and he says, "she's all i ever listen to". and then, "you
kind of remind me of her, you know? you always seem
just a little bit sad. smiling, but sad. i like that..." *(beat)*
the fuck did that mean? you know? because, listen, you
don't say stuff like that to a thirteen-year-old, okay?
you just don't, uh-uh, 'cause she'll be yours for life. i
mean it. if you do, she will be...

(pause)

not in front of my house, but down from it, a block
maybe, he pulls over, there's a florist shop and its
closed, this time of the evening, and he parks in the
little lot they have there...he kissed me. jesus, he kissed
me like, i guess, you imagine how it must've been
when they first invented it, like back in the days of
myths and shit, when, you know, men were heroes and
you could get kissed like that and you'd wait a lifetime

for him to return, you would, and you could still taste
him on your lips, years later, because back then kisses
still meant something, that's what he kissed me like...

*(she takes a sip of water. she fiddles again with the edge of
the water cup but doesn't drink.)*

i really don't wanna, umm, elaborate too much on,
well, you know, cover all the relationship stuff a whole
lot, 'cause if you've talked to him you know it already,
anyway, right? maybe more than you want to... *(beat)*
we started seeing each other, you know, as much as a
junior high school teacher and a thirteen-year-old can
see each other, that's what we began to do. we started
doing that. and i know what you're thinking, or have
thought it to each other, laughing and stuff, that it's
my own fault or that he was some type 'a molester,
whatever, but you wouldn't really be true about that.
either side of that. we, umm...just liked each other. and
would kiss and things, not so much, but kiss and little
hugs and stuff—i'd sneak into his classroom at lunch
for, like, just seconds sometimes, and we'd hug—that's
what we'd do.

(pause)

my fourteenth birthday...'s in march, i'm a pisces...
"the fish". how 'bout that? i guess it was really the
weekend of, the actual day fell on a thursday, but
that saturday, he, umm, picked me up at the library,
the downtown branch, where i did book sorting on a
volunteer basis, 'cause you get a bunch of privileges
and stuff if you do it twice a month...but i told her, the
volunteer coordinator, she was just a high school girl
anyway, i told her i felt sick that day and he picked me
up and we went driving, i asked where but he said,
"it's a surprise", so i sat back in the ol' peugeot, the
sun roof was up, 's a real nice day out, and just kind
'a drifted off to the sound of the wind rushing by.

the wind and billie holiday singing sad on the back
speakers...

(she stops, gathering her thoughts a moment.)

when we got to chicago, he drove straight to the
lake, to this pier where he'd rented a boat for us,
beautiful red speedboat, and god, it was so exciting
for me! he just kept doing things like this, and there's
a picnic basket and it was great, just great...to be out
there, in the water, on this boat with him, it was just
real lovely... *(beat)* he gave me a bracelet, it was all
wrapped up, in wax paper, inside my sandwich! yeah,
you believe that, he'd hollowed out my bread and put
my present inside there, and i loved that, that was just
cute...and i got, ahh, this beautiful, like, picture book
of several greek stories, mostly of euripides, 'cause, see,
he felt euripides was the most, what, "humanistic"...
had, like, the most humanity of the greek writers. he
said he was the one most at war with this... *(beat)* shit,
still can't think of that word, but he was the guy who
was really angry about the world being all fucked up
just because we happened to be mortals...anyhow, it
had a bunch 'a nice drawings and he said i'd like it
even more as i got older... *(beat)* i still have it.

i, umm...found out about the baby, that i was going
to have one, in late april, the twenty-third, i guess,
and i didn't cry. i should've, fucking kid myself, you
know, but sometimes you can go along, years even,
and not feel like you're growing up at all, and then
there's times when you age a ton, like, in a couple 'a
seconds. you know? so, i found out and went straight
to his place, i mean, called first, but went there and we
discussed it all. talked a long time... *(beat)* we talked,
like i said, and, you know, he seemed, and this caught
me, 'cause i didn't know what he'd think, but he
was all excited! not yelling, or all adult and shit, and
said he loved children, could think of nothing better

than having a son or something, said we'd have to be
careful—i mean, we both understood the situation—
but i promised him i wouldn't tell anybody who the
father was, no matter if my dad got really shitty about
it—and he did, believe me—or school, or whatever, i
said i'd keep our secret...we made a pledge together,
there on his sofa, and i kept it. *(beat)* he told me that
day, he said he had to go away for a couple weeks, just
the end of summer, he was finishing up another of his
degrees at delphi, that's a university, and then we'd,
you know, make some plans. *(beat)* that was hard,
'cause i was scared, i'm not gonna pretend i wasn't,
but getting his degree was a big thing, and could help
us, too, he said...and so we talked for awhile, and we
kissed, god, you know for being this big guy, he was
really gentle to me...and then i went home. i went
to my house with our baby inside me, and watched
hogan's heroes on t v, like i did every afternoon. i mean,
what else are you gonna do, right? *(beat)* i just need a
little water...

(she pours a touch more into her cup and sips.)

okay. umm, what else? ahh...when i heard he'd left his
position at school—this was by a fluke, anyway, i was
at the general office during the summer, which was not
that far from our house, bringing them a vaccination
report on my brother, and the lady there, the secretary,
said, "oh, i heard about your arts and sciences teacher
at gardner", my school, "we're sure sorry to lose him,
aren't we?" —i didn't hear much else, really, just that
she said, "well, i suppose they need good teachers
in phoenix as much as they do anywhere..." *(beat)*
but i didn't ask for an address or anything, i didn't,
because i was standing there, in that office, suddenly
standing there, fourteen years old with a baby in me
and this woman yacking on about my brother needing
a german measles booster, and did i know if he'd had

one yet, and i was frozen in time. 's like the heavens
had opened above me, at that very second, and all i
could hear was the universe, this woman in front of me
talking on like i was her godchild and all i could make
out was the howl of the cosmos...and you know what?
it was laughing, it was. all it's attention was suddenly
turned and it was laughing, laughing down at me...

(she stops and slowly lights another cigarette.)

like i said, there's a bunch 'a shit you don't need to
hear twice, and i don't want your sympathy, okay,
i don't, so we'll skip the hardship stuff about when
i did tell my family, and being pulled out 'a school,
the move to my aunt's house...sound familiar? i told
you before, or if i didn't, i meant to...this story's
nothing special, really, practically the only part that's
of any interest is that it happened to me...you know?
(beat) anyways, billie, that's my son, billie, "william",
whatever...was born. a beautiful boy. just quite great,
and although every mom goes off on that, he was.
i mean it. he's great, and, umm, without getting all
shitty about it, i give birth and a bunch 'a years pass.
okay? i did finally make contact with his father, sent a
couple letters, and he wrote me back right away, this
was, ohh, maybe a year, eighteen months later...just
long enough to make him wonder, you know? i was
still only about sixteen at the time, so i guess he was
pretty scared about the whole thing—'s what he said
on paper, anyway—and asked if i could understand,
not forgive...understand. *(beat)* i, ahh, let him know
that our pact was still safe, and this wasn't, like,
some money thing, i just wanted him to have, if he
wouldn't mind so much, a sort 'a relationship with
billie, through the mail or whatever, i knew there
was nothing for us, well, you know, not after that...
but i'd send pictures and stuff, we ended up doing it
through a postal box, and he got to know his son that

way. that's how it happened, a few presents now and
again, and he had a son, and the son's mother loved
him, and kept the secret all while the father was away.
and i know you'll think i'm just talking shit now, but
honestly, if i closed my eyes and thought about it, i
could still feel his kiss on my lips. even then...

(long pause)

the rest you know...on his fourteenth birthday, billie
and me, we rented a car—we were living in utah by
then, out with some relatives at that point—and we
drove to arizona to meet his father, we'd planned this,
the two of us, by letter, and agreed it'd be just the one
time...he was, umm, you know, married by this time,
married and teaching in phoenix, no children, though,
isn't that funny? no kids 'cause his wife had a part of
her uterus, i guess, some thing, that wouldn't work
properly, but they didn't adopt and just kept trying
naturally. over and over. i thought that was the only
real sad part 'a all this—so, it'd just be this once, at a
motel that he'd picked in town. one time when we'd all
sit down and see each other. again, at least, the two of
us, again...

(she fiddles with the edge of the tape player.)

this thing's almost run out...

(she looks up but there is no answer.)

okay. *(beat)* we met at the room. 's a terribly hot day,
at least for december it was, 's how i remember it,
anyway, and we were tired from the travel, but he
was there, as promised, hardly seemed any older,
which kind 'a sucked, i thought, 'cause i'd changed—i
mean, look at me, right?—and it was this big moment
for billie, 's all excited, and we even hugged, and it
was in that second, as he leaned in to kiss my cheek,
his head turned toward me and maybe it was just the
light, the sun coming in the room, but i saw something

there, there in his eyes…he loved this boy, all that
shit he'd said to me years ago, it was true about kids.
he loved 'em. but also…he was satisfied, i could see
that, satisfaction on his face…because he'd gotten
away with it all. that's what i saw, shining in his eyes,
as he moved forward to kiss me. he'd beaten fate…
and gotten away with it. *(beat)* after dinner, we had a
bucket of store-bought chicken in the room, billie got
a couple packages—one was a book of myths, imagine
that—he said he wanted to see us again before we left.
he had to run to school for about an hour, a science
fair, i guess, but he'd be back. he promised he'd be
right back. the last time i saw him, there at the door, he
mentioned that word, that…umm, well, whatever, he
said it and smiled, as he stepped out onto the balcony
he smiled to me and whispered, "maybe it's not our
fault after all. i mean, we're just human, right?"

(pause)

billie was already in the bathroom, we'd driven
straight through, and i could hear the water running.
he was in his bath. god, he loved the tub! since he was
tiny, he loved it. so, i knew he was in there, the water
filling up around him, and "lady day"—'s what he
liked to call billie holiday, 's her nickname, and he
called her that—playing on his tape player. "stormy
weather". i, ahh, went into the room, the bathroom,
and i could see him there, through a little opening in
the liner he had pulled shut, eyes closed and the steam
coming up. he didn't really struggle, couldn't actually,
the shock of it, i suppose, when the recorder first hit
the water…there was really only a quick kind 'a snap-
ping sound, like the pop of a flashbulb or whatnot,
and then the softer sound of him, billie, as he kicked
a second or two in the water. i turned the taps off a
little later… *(beat)* after, i just sat there, on the linoleum,
and watched him, lying in that cloudy pool of bath

water, his eyes open and so still, i thought i could
almost see, i mean, if i squinted, i could almost make
out…"adakia", that's the word. the word i was trying,
you know, that's it. "the world out of balance". you can
look it up if you wanna, but i'm sure that's the one…i
knew it'd come to me, if i waited long enough.

(she lights another smoke.)

i was picked up in vegas, at a restaurant, you're aware
of that, though, obviously…and brought back here.
and that's it. so, now you know. i mean, what you
really wanted, anyway, right? now you know…yes, i
planned it, yes. but…maybe longer than you thought,
huh? lots longer…

(she laughs to herself.)

and i worry about what's gonna happen, i mean, to me
and all, i do—'s natural, though, right, to wonder about
things—but i'll tell you. tell you what gets me through
today, the next hour…it's him. my teacher.

(pause)

i can almost see 'em, you know, i can, down there
in phoenix, probably wandering around on some
playground at school, a saturday, and he's just
stumbling there by himself near the monkey bars. can't
be consoled, right, the truth all spilled out now like it
is, and all these tears running down, yelling up at the
sky, these torrents of tears and screaming, the top of
his lungs, calling up into the universe, "why?! why?!!"
over and over. *(beat)* but you know what? in my
fantasy, there's never an answer, uh-uh, there never
is…

*(she sits and smokes now as the tape player continues to
quietly hum on. silence, darkness)*

END OF PLAY

CPSIA information can be obtained
at www.ICGtesting.com
Printed in the USA
LVHW010518030820
662193LV00011B/1389